AND THEN THERE WERE NONE

by NINA LEEN

with commentary by
JOSEPH A. DAVIS

AND
THEN
THERE
WERE
NONE

America's
Vanishing
Wildlife

HOLT, RINEHART AND WINSTON
New York   Chicago   San Francisco

A Holt Reinforced Edition
Photographs and Preface copyright © 1973 by Nina Leen
Introduction and captions copyright © 1973 by Joseph A. Davis
All rights reserved, including the right to reproduce
this book or portions thereof in any form.
Published simultaneously in Canada by
Holt, Rinehart and Winston of Canada, Limited.

Library of Congress Cataloging in Publication Data

Leen, Nina,
  And then there were none.

  SUMMARY: The Florida manatee, puma, and the bald
eagle are some of the endangered species photographed
and discussed here.

  1. Rare animals. [1. Rare animals. 2. Wildlife
conservation] I. Davis, Joseph Anthony, 1930–
II. Title.
QL88.L43   596   72–91655
ISBN 003–007466–5

Printed in the United States of America
First Edition
Layout by Nina Leen

Contents

Preface

Early in 1972, I was surprised when the editors of Holt, Rinehart and Winston asked me to do a book on the endangered species of the United States. Many books and stories in national magazines were published about animals in danger of extinction in Africa and other faraway places, but pictures of native endangered species seldom appeared. Eagles and whooping cranes were some of the few exceptions publicized. Considering the much photographed exotic competition—who would care to see the U.S. salt marsh harvest mouse, and as a friend assured me, I would never see one either. Thinking of the numerous difficulties and given a time limit (about six months to locate and photograph the animals), it seemed to be a hopeless project—but I respect the little prairie dog as much as the majestic tiger and decided that it was worth trying.

At the beginning I had encouraging responses from wildlife departments, scientists, zoos, wildlife preserves, and many private individuals. From the University of California, Professor Robert C. Stebbins and graduate students Stephen Ruth and Ronald Marlow spent dismal hours with me, in pouring rain, waiting for the Santa Cruz long-toed salamanders to appear after sundown from the surrounding hills. They were conducting a study of the small amphibians and I was allowed to join them. Shooting the pictures with speed-lights in rain was an ordeal but despite the weather and late hours, Stephen and Ronald were surprisingly good natured.

I realize that it will be impossible for me to describe everybody's cooperation in detail—it would easily fill many pages. I would like to thank the people who helped me with advice, permissions, and sometimes gave me a lot of their time. Following are their names and please forgive me if I left somebody out!

Dr. Robert C. Stebbins, Professor of Zoology and Curator of Herpetology, University of California at Berkeley; Stephen

7

B. Ruth and Ronald Marlow, Museum of Vertebrate Zoology, University of California at Berkeley; Norman R. Winnik, Director, Point Defiance Zoo, Tacoma, Washington; Cecil Brosseau, Director, Point Defiance Aquarium, Tacoma, Washington; Chester E. Hogan, Director, Los Angeles Zoo, and Frank S. Todd, Curator of Birds, who introduced me to Topa Topa, the first California condor I ever saw—the only condor in captivity; Kenton C. Lint, Curator of Birds, San Diego Zoo; Howard T. Lee and L. D. Nuckles, Texas Parks and Wildlife Department; Professor Walter W. Dalquest, Department of Biology, Midwestern University, Wichita Falls, Texas; Dr. W. L. Minckley, Assistant Professor, Department of Zoology, Arizona State University, Tempe, Arizona; Jack L. Tinker, Managing Director, and Wayne G. Homan, General Curator, Phoenix Zoo; Walter A. Snyder, Chief of Game Management, New Mexico Department of Game and Fish; Mr. and Mrs. George Hightower, Red Rock, New Mexico; Lawrence Curtis, Director, and Ernest Hagler, Assistant Director, Oklahoma City Zoo; Gordon Hubbel, Director, and Peter Terry, Curator of Birds, Crandon Park Zoo, Miami; Dr. O. E. Frye, Jr., Director, Florida Game and Fresh Water Fish Commission; Jack Watson, Big Paine Key, Florida; Mr. and Mrs. Lester Piper, Everglades Wonder Gardens, Bonita Springs, Florida; The Marineland of Florida; Harold Egoscue, Manager Small Mammals and Primates, Washington National Zoo, Washington, D.C.; Arthur Watson, Director, Baltimore Zoo; Dr. Roger Conant, Director, and J.

Kevin Bowler, Assistant Curator of Reptiles, Philadelphia Zoo; Richard G. Naegeli, Director, Franklin Park Zoo, Boston; Elmer H. Taylor, Curator, and Mrs. Karla Field, New England Aquarium, Boston; Carl Kauffeld, Director, Staten Island Zoo; H. B. House, Curator of Mammals, Wayne King, Curator of Reptiles, New York Zoological Park; Joseph A. Davis, Scientific Assistant to the Director of the New York Zoological Society; Heinz Meng, Department of Biological Sciences, State University College, New Paltz, New York; Dr. Ray C. Erickson, Patuxent Wildlife Research Center, Maryland; Robert Rush Miller, University of Michigan and Chairman, Endangered Species Committee, American Fisheries Society, and Karl Koopman of the American Museum of Natural History in New York City.

I am very grateful to Mrs. Si Merrill, Mr. Leslie Speed, Mr. George A. Matis, and Mr. George Clark.

I can't give a big enough thank you to the people of the Time-Life Lab. Whenever I had problems, they always answered my cries for help.

NINA LEEN

New York City
June 1973

Introduction

Man, the only species of animal to have written books and created conscious works of art is, in addition, the only one known to have brought about the total extinction of other species.

Until a few generations ago, with some exceptions man's influence on Nature was slight and ephemeral; with few exceptions, the land and its wild inhabitants could recover from whatever he did because the effects were only local. But our ancestors occasionally did manage to undo the intricate and millennia-long labors of the evolutionary process by the simple method of overhunting. We can forgive those who went before us their excesses—if we wish—on the grounds that they had no notion of what game biologists call "maximum sustained yield." Today, it should seem elementary to all of us (except some who make commercial use of wildlife) that, if one is to remove animals from the wild, he must not take more in any year than the species can replace through breeding.

The inhabitants of islands are far more vulnerable than those of the continental land masses. The most conspicuous of the reasons for this is the fact that there exists no surrounding area of similar habitat from which replacements can come for the plants and animals man destroys. Dodos could be found in historical times nowhere in the world but on a handful of small islands in the Indian Ocean, and when they had been wiped out on their tiny refuges, no dodo existed anywhere else to rekindle the species. The Hawaiian Islands and some in the Caribbean have already lost dozens of species of animals, and nothing we can do will ever bring them back.

The sea mink, larger than the familiar American mink, disappeared before anyone thought to save a single specimen for a museum. No skin exists today, not even an entire skeleton. No painter has left us so much as a sketch of it. The official date of the sea mink's demise is listed as 1890, but it vanished from its haunts along the

New England coast earlier than that, and the date is, in a sense, merely the legal declaration of its death.

Nine kinds of mammals have been eliminated on our continent since our European ancestors settled here, and all but one of these animals were destroyed within the last 100 years. Six kinds of birds exist no more in North America— or anywhere. The list of our animals which will never be seen again is, perhaps, shorter than it might have been, for we have rescued an occasional species, such as the bison, from the jaws of oblivion. We have lost ten distinctive geographical races of species which still survive as species in other areas, but we have utterly destroyed the sea mink and Steller's sea cow, the great auk, passenger pigeon, and Carolina parakeet as species beyond all possibility of resurrection. We have killed off the wolf and elk in our eastern states and have virtually exterminated the magnificent puma as well. But the remaining members of the races we have not yet destroyed are in almost every case few in number. We have no reason for regarding them as safe.

The larger carnivores have been systematically eliminated in North America because of their supposed threat to human safety and that of domestic livestock. The danger to human life was always more imagined than substantial. It is true that some individual predators did turn to killing the livestock so conveniently penned up in preference to their natural prey, and it was characteristic of human nature to blame all wolves or all pumas rather than to seek out the offend-

ing individual. So many of the big carnivores came crashing down before the inexorable advance of the Frontier.

As the predators were killed around new settlements, so, too, were other species killed to feed the new communities. At the same time land was cleared for agriculture to sustain the settlers, habitat was destroyed without which many kinds of animals could not survive. Millions of passenger pigeons were destroyed, not only by unregulated slaughter at the hands of commercial market hunters, but by the felling of the great forest that once carpeted the east. The wolf and puma disappeared from the same area in part, at least, because their prey, the whitetail deer, was, for a time, all but eliminated from parts of the area. The deer has recovered, perhaps too well, but the predators have not returned, and the deer are the worse for it. Where once the predators culled the weak and the ill-adapted, their human successors generally seek out the finest specimens and leave the weak to breed again.

Two organizations have officially ruled on the status of rare and endangered animals: Species found on the North American continent (and in Hawaii) have been categorized by the U.S. Department of the Interior; the International Union for the Conservation of Nature and Natural Resources (IUCN) generally accepts the Department of the Interior's designations but covers the animals of the rest of the world as well. Both of these organizations tend to be conservative in judging rarity or endangerment. Exclusion from their listings does not imply that a species is in no danger, but those who derive economic gain from the exploitation of wildlife often try to give that impression.

In the pages that follow, we have chosen species according to less stringent criteria. The official "endangered" category requires a status so critical that one might consider the species terminal, barring heroic, and perhaps miraculous, intervention on our part. The California condor is such a species. By official criteria, the sea otters of the California coast are merely "rare"; they exist in small enough numbers (something over 1000) that a worsening of the environment could seriously endanger them. There was a time when a moratorium on hunting could provide all the protection needed by such a species, but that time ended with the advent of large-scale multiple environmental degradation. Without lifting a firearm or setting a snare, we can doom the California brown pelican. We can doom it in the name of protecting the cotton crop from insect pests by using insecticides and never know what we have done until it is too late.

In our world of accelerating technological change, a species can slide from rare to endangered in far less time than it takes for the official designation to be changed. Worse, it can make the transition before it even reaches the rare category officially. Smaller species or races might even become extinct without ever being discovered.

None of the animals pictured in this book need to become extinct. Action has been initiated in behalf of many of them already. Some of it began decades ago; some is of very recent origin. At all levels, government is beginning to shoulder its responsibilities toward the environment and the animals which are a part of it. Conservation organizations are increasingly active.

The final power to save or destroy our wildlife lies in the hands of all of us. But the choices are not clear-cut. We may have to accept some insect damage to the food we eat if we are to keep the eagles. We may have to put up with the annoyance of mosquitoes if we are to preserve the viable wetlands that are necessary to the lives of so many species. Our towns may have to make sacrifices in order to provide more open space for its wildlife. We may have to accept higher prices for things made in a less polluting fashion, and we may have to live less wastefully. Some of us know that we will be the richer for doing without many of the antibiological things that we have been trained to consider essential to our way of life. A great many others have yet to learn the lesson.

JOSEPH A. DAVIS

Bloomingdale, New Jersey
June 1973

AND THEN THERE WERE NONE

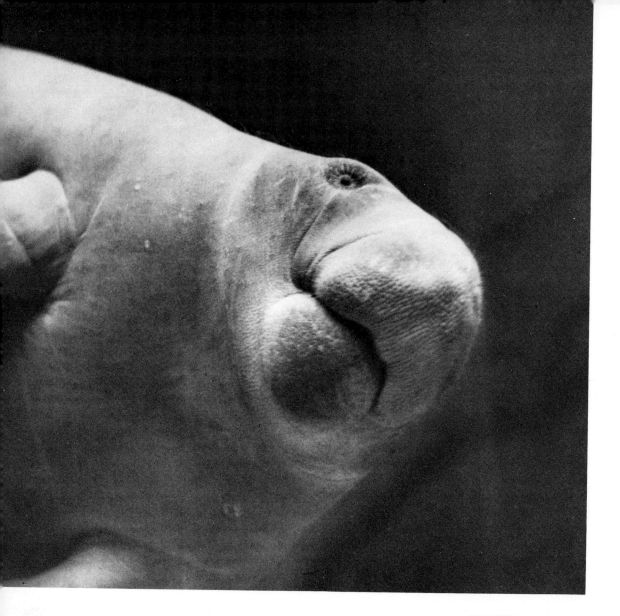

FLORIDA MANATEE

The manatee's precarious tenancy of the southern part of Florida is jeopardized not only by dangers of human encroachment. The occasional hard freezes that hit the area chill this sea cow's watery home enough to be fatal. Everything in its makeup fits it for the life of a sluggish, underwater grazer. Like all aquatic mammals, it seals off its nostrils by muscular constriction while it is below the surface (right).

All mammals require air. At left, the manatee
returns to the surface to breathe. Like the
whales, manatees long ago lost their hind limbs
and opted for a totally aquatic existence. In their
element, they are exquisitely graceful despite
their bulk, which can measure up to half a ton.

FLORIDA PUMA

The puma was one of the most successful predators of recent times. It ranged as a species from Canada southward through the equatorial regions of South America to the cold lands of southern Argentina. But because it is a large animal and a predator, European settlers exterminated it from most of the North American continent. A few pumas still survive in the Maritime Provinces of Canada and in the Everglades of Florida. It has been so widespread that it was given many names—cougar, mountain lion, cat-o'mountain, panther, to name a few.

This young Florida puma, seen with its mother, doesn't need human help to survive. It needs only freedom from human harassment. When cubs are young the mother does not roam around; she stays with them in a well-concealed den.

The puma hunts by night as well as by day.

KEY DEER

As it spread throughout most of North America,
the adaptable whitetail deer was shaped locally
by many new environments. In the Florida Keys,
a diminutive race of the whitetail arose, less than
2½ feet tall at the shoulder. Although it is
relatively safe from hunting, the Key deer is
threatened by dogs and by automobiles.

The buck, bearing antlers, and the doe, lying down, are among some 300 Key deer surviving in Florida. In 1949, there were only thirty Key deer known in existence. The race is far from safe, as real estate development increases.

SOUTHERN BALD EAGLE

The bald eagle, our national symbol, is beset by
many dangers in the United States. An increasing
human population is preempting or disrupting
nesting sites, and the birds are still being shot
illegally. Accumulating persistent pesticides and
other contaminants have interfered with the
reproductive physiology of this and other
predatory species.

The great horned owl, sporting hornlike tufts
of feathers, and the great gray owl with
its feathery, round face are comparatively
safe from hunters, but like all predatory birds,
they are at the mercy of certain chemicals
which prevail in our environment and are
concentrated in species on which they feed.

Ruin of a Desert Habitat

The Texas kangaroo rat evolved in an arid
habitat which, seemingly desolate, can support
animals in limited numbers. To the detriment of
these desert rodents, mesquite and other plants
on which they feed have been bulldozed away.
Extensive modification of the extremely limited
range of the Texas kangaroo rat has seriously
endangered this little rodent.

TEXAS KANGAROO RAT

When seeds are plentiful, the kangaroo rat stores and cures enormous quantities of food for the future. It can metabolize water from the carbohydrates in the seeds, and thereby survive without ever drinking.

Although most snakes are beneficial to man, a few species are also poisonous; ignorance and fear of them prompt indiscriminate slaughter. Both the venomous ridge-nosed rattlesnake (below) and the inoffensive indigo snake (top, right) are very important in the balance of nature. Overcollecting and habitat destruction also endanger their survival. The extremely limited habitat of the San Francisco garter snake (below, right) is being filled with housing developments.

DESERT BIGHORNS

Desert bighorn sheep have lived for thousands of
years in small populations on mountain "islands"
in an otherwise hostile sea of sand. Overhunting
and disease brought in by herds of domesticated
sheep, preempting their habitat, have reduced the
wild sheep numbers to a mere handful. With
protection and transplanting of nucleus herds to
former habitats, the desert bighorns can begin once
more to fill their unique role in the environment.

These bighorn ewes have been brought to Red
Rock, New Mexico, for release into the wild
once they have become acclimated.

Only a few days old, this bighorn lamb, one of four born to the ewes shipped to Red Rock, is already capable of following its mother. It spends much of its time exploring and resting.

Threatened Wetlands

The intricate water and wildlife system of the Everglades, south Florida's last stronghold of protected nature, is greatly threatened by proposed roads and housing developments. Big Cypress Swamp, a complex storage area of water on which the Everglades depends for its flow of water, contains approximately twenty rare or endangered species as well as many other unique plants and wild animals. More than half its water supply comes from the Big Cypress. Many tropical plants growing in the Everglades cannot be found anywhere else in the continental United States. The Everglades, the "river of grass," is in increasing danger from fires (canals which drain the land and result in extensive fire are constantly dug by developers). The proposed interstate highway which may run through Big Cypress could be a tragic blow to Everglades National Park and all its wildlife.

AMERICAN CROCODILE

The American crocodile reaches its northernmost
limits in the southern tip of Florida in the
Everglades. The posture it assumes here—with
open mouth—is a characteristic resting pose.
The crocodile is far more rare in the United
States than the alligator.

AMERICAN ALLIGATOR

The alligator's habit of digging deep holes in
times of drought provides water and living space
for fishes, frogs, and other small animals. The
'gator does not hesitate to dine on its guests, but
enough survive because of the waterholes to
perpetuate their species.

The young alligator shown here still has much of
the contrasting light markings of its youth.
By maturity, the 'gator's back will become
almost uniformly dark, while the belly remains
pale. The alligator's blunt snout distinguishes
it from the American crocodile.

WHOOPING CRANE

The whooping crane's slow comeback is far from the point at
which conservationists can relax. The birds must fly 2400 miles
twice each year between their summer nesting grounds in the
MacKenzie District of Canada and the Gulf Coast of Texas where
they winter. Wildlife biologists keep a careful count of the cranes
at both ends of their route. The birds are on the increase, but in
the winter of 1972, ten failed to return to their wintering grounds.

A pair of cranes are followed by their nearly
grown offspring in the Aransas Refuge in Texas.
Dredging operations have nearly undone years
of patient protection for these large birds.

In this series, the parent whooping cranes indulge in preflight movements as their chick walks ahead. The chick flaps its wings, then takes flight behind its parents.

TULE ELK

The Tule, the smallest of the races of elk,
now exists in California in three herds, totaling
about 400 animals. Miners in the Gold Rush days
hunted it nearly to extinction, but the elk's
greatest recent danger lies in man's intrusion
on its habitat.

SALT MARSH HARVEST MOUSE

The salt marsh harvest mouse, also of California,
is another casualty of human expansion in its
San Francisco Bay home. Since mice are harder
to census than elk, it is not possible to tell how
bad its situation is. New bans on development
in the Bay wetlands may save it.

DESERT TORTOISE

The desert tortoise's greatest threat is the pet trade. As is the case with almost all desert creatures, the tortoise exists in low population densities, and a determined collector can have a devastating effect.

BOG TURTLE

The bog turtle of the northeastern states is also beleaguered by collectors, for the turtle commands high prices because of its rarity. The usurpation of its restricted wetland habitat by the sprawling suburbs, however, is its major threat.

SEA TURTLES

Both the Atlantic Ridley (left) and the young
Green turtle (below) are seriously reduced in
numbers. Turtle meat is still a delicacy and the
oil is used in some cosmetics. The turtles lay
their eggs on Caribbean beaches where, once
relatively safe from predators, they are now dug
up by man for gourmet food.

CALIFORNIA CONDOR

There is some question as to how much longer the California condor's 9-foot wingspan will cast its shadow on the landscape. Sensitive to human disturbance, the slow-breeding condor's numbers are declining steadily. Some are still being shot illegally, and now-illegal poison baits, left for coyotes, may be taking an additional toll. Sanctuaries have been established, but they may not be extensive enough to meet the bird's exacting requirements. This young condor will require several years until it reaches breeding age.

SPOTTED BAT

The spotted bat of the Southwest has always
been so rare that almost nothing is known of
its life history. Little can be done to protect
it until we know what its biological needs are.
Like all insect-eating bats, it is probably
threatened by the use of persistent pesticides.

BLACK-FOOTED FERRET

The black-footed ferret probably was never very common, even
in the old prairie dog towns that were measured by the square
mile. As poison campaigns directed against the rodents caused the
dog towns to diminish and then disappear from lands converted
to agricultural use, the ferret appears to have faded away as well.
It can subsist on other prey, but it seems to need the burrow
systems excavated by the prairie dogs for its own dens. The
Department of the Interior now has a program investigating the
characteristics of the ferret at the Patuxent Wildlife Research
Center in Maryland. In addition to yielding valuable information
on the biological needs and other management needs of the
species, the project could result in techniques for raising ferrets
for release in their former habitat. The Patuxent Wildlife
Research Center, where the pictures on these pages were taken,
has the only three black-footed ferrets known in captivity today.

UTAH PRAIRIE DOG

The Utah whitetail prairie dog occupies only a small range and may never have been abundant. Because it can be a carrier of sylvatic plague, eradication programs destroyed numbers of these rodents. Now government control measures have been discontinued, but because agriculture and prairie dogs are not compatible, the species will be fortunate if it can hold even its present habitat.

The busy social life in the prairie dog community is exciting and varied. At left, a minor squabble is followed by retreat. Here, two prairie dogs approach, then "kiss," a form of friendly contact or recognition.

KIT FOX

Kit foxes are quite unwary compared with other foxes. Poisons and traps, set out in misguided efforts to control rodents or coyotes, take a heavy toll on these graceful little carnivores. In many parts of their western range, kit foxes have become quite rare.

MOHAVE CHUB

The Mohave chub today occupies only a small
part of its original range along the Mohave River
in southern California. Another species of chub,
introduced into the river by man, has interbred
with this native species and has thereby destroyed
it as a species almost everywhere.

WOUNDFIN

The small woundfin can live only in swiftly flowing, silt-laden waters. Projected dams in the lower Colorado Basin threaten to change almost all of this fish's habitat into unsuitable waters. Even now, present dams and rerouted rivers have taken their toll.

Decline of a River

The Hudson River, near Hastings, New York,
where the fisherman sets out at dawn, has seen
changes in its fish fauna. The shortnose
sturgeon, for example, is rarely encountered now.
Not long ago this river was one of the most
beautiful in the world. Today, industrial waste,
sewage, and other pollutants threaten the
survival of this picturesque waterway.

ATLANTIC STURGEON

The Atlantic sturgeon is one of the most ancient
of bony fishes, a survivor of countless geological
changes. Commercial value and the fouling of
rivers in which they spawn have combined
to imperil many of our larger fishes. This
species may reach 12 feet but is slow to
mature and probably does not spawn every year.

LAKE STURGEON

Like its relatives, the lake sturgeon of the Great
Lakes region is a bottom feeder. Its long,
whiskerlike feelers enable it to locate small
organisms as it moves along the lake floor.
When it touches food, the sturgeon's mouth
protrudes and sucks up the morsel. Of the seven
species of sturgeon found in the United
States, the lake sturgeon is the most desirable
in the commercial market and overfishing
has reduced its numbers severely.

SEA OTTER

The sea otter has had one close brush with
extinction at the hands of man, and, with man's
more recent protection, has grown to what
should be a healthy number. Over 1000 sea
otters inhabit the kelp beds of the California
coast, but abalone fishermen consider them
competitors, and bullet-riddled carcasses are not
uncommonly found. Amchitka Island, in the
Aleutian chain, in whose waters lives one of the
largest concentrations of otters, has already been
used as a testing ground for nuclear devices; the
1971 blast killed 1000 otters, and the possibility
that radioactive wastes will leach into the
sea is an even more serious threat.

Lacking blubber under its skin, the sea otter
depends on its dense fur to insulate it from the
cold. The otter above is grooming its fur, an
occupation that fills much of its waking hours.

By dining on sea urchins, a
favorite food, the otter helps to
protect the kelp. Kelp forests
provide shelter for the otters
and for abalones. Otters'
predation on urchins is necessary
for the abalones' survival.

ROSEATE SPOONBILL

Plume hunters devastated many of our larger
birds of the wetlands, but protective laws have
enabled most to recover. Now the "reclamation"
of wetlands has reduced much of their habitat,
and a new crisis looms. The roseate spoonbill
reaches its northern limits in the Gulf
States but is still found throughout much of
South America.

GREAT WHITE HERON

Here a great white heron waits on its favorite rock for small fishes to swim into range. Hurricanes are a particular danger to this species—40% of the Florida population died in hurricane Donna in 1960. Fortunately, the heron's recuperative powers are good and, in three years, the losses had been made up. The total population, however, is not large.

EASTERN BROWN PELICAN

The brown pelican is widely distributed along much of the coastlines of North and South America. Pesticide residues have seriously decreased the reproductive capacities of those pelicans in the United States' waters. Photographed in Florida, the young eastern pelican (in the foreground below) has not yet attained its adult coloration. At right, an adult preens its feathers with its remarkable beak.

CALIFORNIA BROWN PELICAN

California brown pelicans have had little breeding success in
recent years because pesticide residues caused them to lay eggs
with shells too thin and weak to survive incubation. These two
young birds, photographed at the Los Angeles Zoo where they
were being treated, are the only survivors of 38 found
with an intestinal ailment.

KODIAK BEAR

Because of their sedentary nature and the mountainous terrain of western North America, brown bears tend to form small populations with similar physical traits, leading early zoologists to name each new group as a new species or race. Actually, as different as their faces seem, the bears in the photo (below) belong to one race of brown bear, from Kodiak Island, Alaska. Kodiak bears are the largest living land carnivores in the world. Despite the show of teeth, the bears at the right are merely playing.

9369

GRIZZLY BEAR

Grizzly bears belong to the same species as the brown bear, but their frosted hair makes them look quite different. Within a grizzly population, variations in the degree of frosting often give individual bears a wide range of appearances. Grizzlies have been shot and trapped since their discovery by early explorers.

POLAR BEAR

Polar bears evolved in a region inhospitable
to man. They are strong swimmers and their
hairy soles facilitate walking on ice.
Aircraft and high-powered rifles now make
man a serious enemy in a region that was
once safe for these bears.

WOOD IBIS

Another species whose destiny is tied
to the future of wetlands is the wood
ibis, the only stork found in the United
States. The wood ibises on the left
have joined in group sunning in a
treetop which is a characteristic habit.
The rough-looking, naked head is a
sign of maturity.

The marshlands along the Tamiami Trail hold an abundance of small creatures on which the ibis feeds. At the right is a young ibis, with feathers still clinging to its head and neck.

RED WOLF

The red wolf, a species of the southern United States, is very close to extinction. In addition to the expectable threats of overhunting and poisoning, a biological danger looms large. The red wolf interbreeds with coyotes and domestic dogs, adulterating its heritage with alien genes. The animal at the left appears to have some coyote blood.

EASTERN TIMBER WOLF

The timber wolf has little chance for survival in the United States
unless old, persistent prejudices disappear first. Even in sparsely
populated Alaska and Quebec, backward attitudes still permit
serious overhunting, despite the fact that the wolf is necessary
for the long-term well-being of the deer on which it preys.
Howling is a form of communication between wolves.

DELMARVA PENINSULA FOX SQUIRREL

This Delmarva fox squirrel's means of existence
is being usurped by land development on the
peninsula where Maryland, Delaware, and
Virginia meet. Without the protection of
refuges, this large relative of the gray
squirrel will become extinct.

A Wetland Saved

FLORIDA SANDHILL CRANE

Corkscrew Swamp in the National Audubon
Society's Sanctuary is one of the largest habitats
of the Florida sandhill crane. Never plentiful,
its occurrence is spotty, and as its needed
environment diminishes, so will the crane.
Florida's cranes are protected by both federal
and state laws.

MISSISSIPPI SANDHILL CRANE

The Mississippi sandhill cranes face
the same problems as their Florida
relatives. Protection of the marshes in
which cranes nest will help, as will a
ban on the hunting of this extremely
endangered species.

A large bird, the sandhill crane reaches 4 feet in maturity with a wingspread of 7 feet. It is quite gregarious and indulges in delightful display as evidenced by the remarkable series of photographs seen here.

MASKED BOBWHITE

The masked bobwhite was ousted from its
foothold in southern Arizona early in this
century. Now it lives only in a few isolated bits
of grassland in the neighboring Mexican state of
Sonora, where cattle have not yet overgrazed the
land. New efforts at rearing the birds in captivity
and the setting aside of suitable land in Arizona
on which to release them may reestablish this
dark bobwhite in the United States.

GILA MONSTER

Sparsely distributed over a harsh desert environment, the Gila monster, one of the world's two venomous lizards, has been a prized catch for pet dealers. Its status is not known with certainty, though it is among the endangered.

JAGUAR

Some of the more spectacular of our
animals have included the United
States only marginally in their ranges
in recent times. Jaguars that stray
across the border from Mexico have
slim prospects of surviving unhunted
for any length of time. Elsewhere in
the Americas, the jaguar has been
overhunted for its pelt. New state and
federal bans on the importation of
jaguar skins—by closing the United
States market—may lessen hunting
pressure in the wild.

COATI

The coati occupies a bit more of the Southwest than the jaguar does, but its small size and inconspicuous nature allows it to coexist with man. This young coati, barely weaned, is already adept at the climbing and leaping its way of life demands.

WOODLAND CARIBOU

Overhunting has cut down the range of the woodland caribou drastically. Now found in sparsely scattered parts of their former territory, a broad belt across southern Canada and the most northern areas of the United States, this race needs protection perhaps more than those more northern populations which are less subject to human predation. The fawn at left, several days old, is already nosing about on the ground in search of plants on which to nibble. Like all new fawns, it spends much of the day resting (below, right).

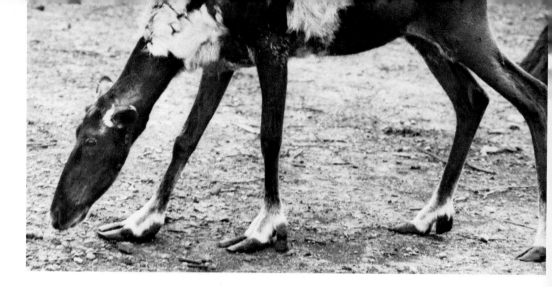

The moth-eaten look of the female above is due to no disease but is part of the annual springtime sloughing off of her dense winter coat. Her broad hoofs, even more noticeable now that the legs are clothed in short hair, make it possible for the deer to traverse snow and soft ground; they are, in effect, snowshoes, clumsy looking, but effective.

THICK-BILLED PARROT

The thick-billed parrot was at times an abundant visitor to the mountains of the extreme Southwest. Expanding human population in Mexico, with extensive cutting of the parrot's forest habitat, is no doubt the root of its trouble. It may already be too late to save enough forest to sustain the species.

MARGAY

The handsome margay, like the larger ocelot, occasionally wanders north into the United States from Mexico. Although the market for its pelt has been essentially stopped by legislation in this country, the demand for the margay in Europe still poses a grave threat to this American cat.

SONORAN GREEN TOAD

The little Sonoran green toad hides from the sun by day in its diminishing habitat in Arizona and Sonora. It breeds in rainwater pools in the cool of the night.

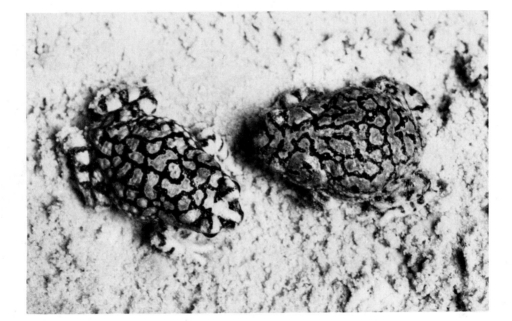

PINE BARRENS TREE FROG

The Pine Barrens tree frog (right) has the misfortune of living in an area with high real estate values. A large jetport, narrowly averted in the Pine Barrens of New Jersey, could have spelled the end of the main population of this specialized frog along with other species found only in this unique area.

The Environmental Impact of a Highway

Ten thousand years ago—perhaps twice as far back in time—the moist climate that covered California began to grow drier and more inhospitable to those salamanders that had taken up residence there. Three hundred miles to the north of Santa Cruz County and 150 miles to the northeast, the mountains remained wet enough for the species, but the growing aridity at Santa Cruz forced its long-toed salamanders into ever smaller pockets of still-suitable habitat.

The existence of this relict race was discovered only in 1954, by which time the salamanders were found to live near and, more important, breed in two ponds four miles apart. Fifteen years later, the larger pond, Valencia Lagoon, was all but destroyed with the widening of U.S. 1 by the California Highway Department, and a drainage channel constructed next to the highway drained much of what was left of the wet area. When the situation was explained to them, the Highway Department set about to reconstruct what was left of the pond, but it is questionable whether the salamanders will use the made-over pond (left). They had not done so in the breeding season of 1971.

SANTA CRUZ LONG-TOED SALAMANDER

The smaller pond, located at Ellicott Station, after a long drought, began to fill again with the rains of 1972. Careful checking of a "salamander corral" put up around the pond by herpetologists disclosed that the amphibians came to the water from the hills at the right of the photo above.

Two salamanders, probably both males, arrive at
the pond as the rain begins. Females generally
come on the scene later, after the males are out
in force. The eggs are attached to the submerged
parts of water plants growing at the edges
of the shallow pond (right).

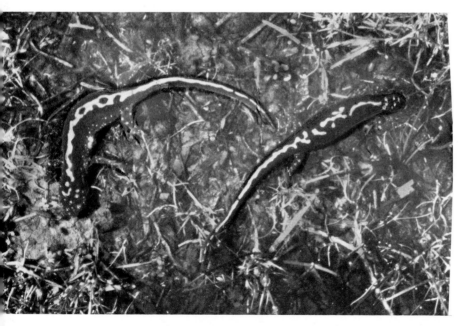

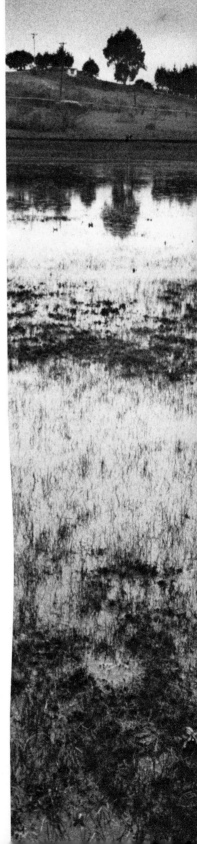

A Breakthrough in Captive Breeding

The peregrine falcon no longer breeds east of the Mississippi River. The same chemical perils that affect the eagles seem to be at work against the falcon, but other factors are at work, too. It is still shot at, and its nesting places are subject to easy disturbance. Until recently, peregrines never bred in captivity. Now two new breakthroughs have occurred almost simultaneously.
Scientists at Cornell University have succeeded in producing peregrine chicks from eggs fertilized by artificial insemination. A biologist at the State University of New York at New Paltz, Dr. Heinz Meng, succeeded in getting a pair of peregrines to breed on their own. In both cases, the result was the same—a falcon chick beginning to chip its way out of the egg.

PEREGRINE FALCON

The time from pipping—the initial opening pecked by the chick—and hatching can span more than two full days.

As the female falcon defends her nest, she not only looks threatening, but she can, in fact, drive off all but the most determined interloper.

At night, Dr. Meng hand feeds his second full
brood of peregrines. The babies have a seemingly
insatiable capacity for food; when at last their
crops are distended, they drop off to sleep until
the next feeding, two hours later.

Feathers are beginning to show through the
down; the falcon is growing.

Above, two of the young peregrines, well feathered, are being trained by Dr. Meng. The female peregrine laid her third successful clutch of eggs in 1972.

The wise man must be wise before, not after, the event.

EPICHARMUS
circa 500 B.C.

Appendix I

Threatened Wildlife of the United States

FISHES

Shortnose sturgeon
Lake sturgeon
Longjaw cisco
Deepwater cisco
Blackfin cisco
Arctic grayling
Lahontan cutthroat trout
Paiute cutthroat trout
Greenback cutthroat trout
Rio Grande cutthroat trout
Humboldt cutthroat trout
Little Kern golden trout
Gila trout
Arizona (Apache) trout
Sunapee trout
Blueback trout
Olympic mudminnow
Desert dace
Humpback chub
Pahranagat bonytail
Mohave chub
Little Colorado spinedace
Moapa dace
Woundfin
Colorado squawfish
Kendall Warm Springs dace
White River (Mountain) sucker
Modoc sucker
Cui-ui
Ozark cavefish
Devil's Hole pupfish
Comanche Springs pupfish
Tecopa pupfish
Nevada pupfish
Warm Springs pupfish
Owens pupfish
Pahrump killifish
Big Bend gambusia
Clear Creek gambusia
Pecos gambusia
San Marcos gambusia

Gila topminnow
Unarmored threespine stickleback
Roanoke bass
Suwannee bass
Sharphead darter
Fountain darter
Niangua darter
Watercress darter
Okaloosa darter
Maryland darter
Trispot darter
Tuscumbia darter
Blue pike
Pygmy sculpin

REPTILES AND AMPHIBIANS

Santa Cruz long-toed salamander
Desert slender salamander
Tehachapi slender salamander
Limestone salamander
Shasta salamander
Jemez Mountain salamander
Texas blind salamander
Black toad, Inyo County toad
Vegas Valley Leopard frog
Houston toad
Pine Barrens tree frog
American crocodile
American alligator
Bog turtle
Green turtle
St. Croix ground lizard
Blunt-nosed leopard lizard
Puerto Rican boa (Culebra Grande)
San Francisco garter snake

Compiled by the Office of Endangered Species and International Activities, Bureau of Sport Fisheries and Wildlife, U.S. Department of the Interior. Published by the Bureau of Sport Fisheries and Wildlife, March, 1973.

BIRDS

Newell's Manx shearwater
Hawaiian dark-rumped petrel (uau)
Eastern brown pelican
California brown pelican
Florida great white heron
Hawaiian goose (nene)
Aleutian Canada goose
Tule white-fronted goose
Laysan duck
Hawaiian duck (koloa)
Mexican duck
California condor
Florida Everglade kite (Florida snail kite)
Puerto Rican sharp-shinned hawk
Hawaiian hawk (io)
Southern bald eagle
Prairie falcon
American peregrine falcon
Arctic peregrine falcon
Northern greater prairie chicken
Attwater's greater prairie chicken
Lesser prairie chicken
Masked bobwhite
Whooping crane
Florida sandhill crane
Mississippi sandhill crane
California clapper rail
Light-footed clapper rail
Yuma clapper rail
California black rail
Hawaiian gallinule (alae ula)
Hawaiian coot (alae keokeo)
Eskimo curlew
Hawaiian stilt (aeo)
California least tern
Puerto Rican plain pigeon
Puerto Rican parrot
Newton's Puerto Rican screech owl
Spotted owl
Puerto Rican whip-poor-will
Red-cockaded woodpecker
American ivory-billed woodpecker
Hawaiian crow (alala)
Small Kauai thrush (puaiohi)
Large Kauai thrush (Kauai omao)
Molokai thrush (olomau)

Nihoa miller bird
Kauai oo (oo aa)
Bachman's warbler
Golden-cheeked warbler
Kirtland's warbler
Elfin Woods warbler
Crested honeycreeper (akohekohe)
Kauai akialoa
Kauai nukupuu
Maui nukupuu
Akiapolaau
Hawaii akepa (akepa)
Maui akepa (akepuie)
Oahu creeper (alauwahio)
Molokai creeper (kakawahie)
Maui parrotbill
Ou
Laysan finch
Nihoa finch
Palila
Wallowa gray-crowned rosy finch
Ipswich sparrow
Dusky seaside sparrow
Cape Sable sparrow

MAMMALS

Indiana bat
Ozark big-eared bat
Virginia big-eared bat
Hawaiian hoary bat
Spotted bat
Utah prairie dog
Kaibab squirrel
Delmarva Peninsula (Bryant) fox squirrel
Everglades fox squirrel
Morro Bay kangaroo rat
Salt marsh harvest mouse
Key Largo wood rat
Block Island meadow vole
Beach meadow vole
Whales
   Sperm whale or Cachalot
   Gray whale
   Blue whale
   Finback whale
   Sei whale

Humpback whale
Right whale
Bowhead whale
Northern Rocky Mountain wolf
Eastern timber wolf
Mexican wolf
Red wolf
San Joaquin kit fox
Glacier bear
Grizzly bear
Black-footed ferret
Southern sea otter
Florida puma
Eastern cougar
Ribbon seal
Caribbean monk seal
Hawaiian monk seal
Guadalupe fur seal
Florida manatee (sea cow)
Tule elk
Key deer

Columbian whitetail deer
Sonoran pronghorn
California bighorn
Peninsular bighorn

PERIPHERAL MAMMALS

A peripheral species or subspecies is one whose occurrence in the United States is at the edge of its natural range and which is threatened with extinction within the United States, although not in its range as a whole.

Coati
Jaguar
Jaguarundi
Ocelot
Margay
Woodland caribou
Mountain caribou

Appendix II

Extinct or Presumed Extinct Wildlife of the United States

FISHES

San Gorgonio trout, *Salmo evermanni*. Santa Ana River in California. Extinct about 1935.

Pahranagat spinedace, *Lepidomeda altivelis*. Outflow of Ash Spring and chain of lakes in the Pahranagat Valley in Nevada. Extinct between 1938 and 1959.

Big Spring spinedace, *Lepidomeda mollispinis pratensis*. Spring-fed marsh, Lincoln County, Nevada. Extinct between 1938 and 1959.

Harelip sucker, *Lagochila lacera*. Found in a few clear streams of the upper Mississippi Valley; Scioto River in Ohio, Tennessee River in Georgia, and the White River in Arkansas; also in the Lake Erie drainage, Blanchard and Auglaize rivers in northwestern Ohio. Not seen since 1900.

Leon Springs pupfish, *Cyprinodon bovinus*. Leon Springs, Pecos County, Texas. Not seen since 1938.

Ash Meadows springfish, *Empetrichthys merriami*. Isolated waters of Death Valley in southern Nevada. Not seen since 1942.

BIRDS

Labrador duck. *Camptorhynchus labradorium*. Northeastern North America. Extinct about 1875. Reason unknown.

Heath hen, *Tympanuchus cupido cupido*. Eastern United States. Extinct in 1932. Reasons—overhunting and loss of habitat.

Great auk, *Pinguinus impennis*. North Atlantic Ocean. Extinct about 1844. Reason—overhunting.

Passenger pigeon, *Ectopistes migratorius*. North American. Extinct in 1914. Reasons—overhunting and loss of habitat.

Culebra Puerto Rican parrot, *Amazona vitata gracilipes*. Culebra Island, Puerto Rico. Extinct about 1899. Reason—unknown.

Mauge's parakeet, *Aratinga chloroptera maugei*. Puerto Rico. Extinct about 1892. Reason—destruction of forest habitat.

Carolina parakeet, *Conuropsis carolinensis carolinensis*. Southeastern United States. Extinct about 1920. Reasons—overhunting and loss of forest habitat.

Louisiana parakeet, *Conuropsis carolinensis ludoviciana*. South central United States. Extinct about 1912. Reasons—overhunting and loss of forest habitat.

In addition, twenty-four species of birds native to Hawaii have become extinct since 1825 due to alteration of environment by modern man.

MAMMALS

Gull Island vole, *Microtus nesophilus*. Gull Island, Long Island Sound, New York. Extinct in 1898.

Amargosa meadow vole, *Microtus californicus scirpensis*. California. Extinct in 1917.

Plains wolf, *Canis lupus nubilus*. Great Plains. Extinct in 1926.

Sea mink, *Mustela macrodon*. New England coast. Extinct in 1890.

Steller's sea cow, *Hydrodamalis stelleri*. North Pacific, Bering Sea. Extinct in 1768.

Eastern elk, *Cervus canadensis canadensis*. United States east of Great Plains. Extinct in 1880.

Merriam elk, *Cervus merriami*. Arizona. Extinct in 1900.

Badlands bighorn, *Ovis canadensis auduboni*. North and South Dakota. Extinct in 1910.

Appendix III

Conservation and Environmental Action Organizations

Friends of the Earth
30 East 42nd Street
New York, New York 10017

National Audubon Society
1130 Fifth Avenue
New York, New York 10028

National Wildlife Federation*
1412 16th Street, N.W.
Washington, D.C. 20036

New York Zoological Society
Bronx Park
Bronx, New York 10460

National Recreation & Park Association
1700 Pennsylvania Avenue, N.W.
Washington, D.C. 20006

*For a complete listing of local and national organizations concerned with environmental action and conservation, write to the National Wildlife Federation for their *Conservation Directory*, $1.50 per copy.

Natural Science for Youth Foundation
763 Silvermine Road
New Canaan, Connecticut 06840

Sierra Club
1050 Mills Tower
San Francisco, California 94104

The Nature Conservancy
1522 K Street, N.W.
Washington, D.C. 20005

The Conservation Foundation
1250 Connecticut Avenue, N.W.
Washington, D.C. 20036

League of Women Voters of the United States
1730 M Street, N.W.
Washington, D.C. 20036

The Izaak Walton League of America
1326 Waukegan Road
Glenview, Illinois 60025